Facilitator's Guide

# The Story of God
## EXPLORING THE BIBLICAL NARRATIVE

BEACON HILL PRESS
OF KANSAS CITY

**Writer/Editor**
Mike L. Wonch
**Director of Curriculum**
Merritt J. Nielson
**Director of Editorial**
Bonnie Perry

The internet addresses, email addresses, and phone numbers in this book are accurate at the time of publication. They are provided as a resource. Beacon Hill Press does not endorse them or vouch for their content or permanence.

Copyright © 2014 by Beacon Hill Press of Kansas City
Beacon Hill Press of Kansas City
PO Box 419527
Kansas City, MO 64141
nph.com

ISBN: 978-0-8341-3350-1
Printed in the
United States of America

10 9 8 7 6 5 4 3 2 1

# TABLE OF CONTENTS

# USING THIS FACILITATOR'S GUIDE

The purpose of this facilitator's guide is to help you lead people into community as they grow in Christ by studying the Word.

## TAKE A LOOK

1. Before you begin to prepare for the first session, get an overview of the entire study. This will enable you to:

- Understand the direction of each session and the overall purpose of the study.
- Know what your group will be reading and studying each week.
- Begin to think and plan what you would like to accomplish by doing this study.

2. Before you teach each session,

- Read over your Facilitator's Guide session for that week, several times, prior to your small group meeting. This will help you become familiar with questions, activities, options, and so on.
- Gather any needed materials.
- Pray for God's direction.

## THE SESSIONS

Each session contains:

- *Opening Our Minds*—the introductory material relevant to the topic for the session.
- *Opening the Word*—the Bible study portion of the session.
- *Opening Our Hearts*—the opportunity for the group to understand how the truth discovered during the session applies to their lives.
- *Imaginative Option*—an activity option to bring extra creativity to your session.
- *Connect*—each week you will have the opportunity to send your class a text and/or email update of what you will study in the upcoming

week. We have provided the weekly text for you to use each week and is designed to be sent to your group the week prior to the session. You can use the message provided as is, or feel free to edit and add your own words to meet the needs of your particular group.

## INVOLVE EVERYONE

We design the questions and activities to enable everyone to participate. Here are some things to keep in mind as you lead your small group:

1. Adults are more interested when they are participants instead of spectators.
2. They'll remember more of what they discuss and do together than what is said in a lecture.
3. When participants get involved in a discussion, be affirming and encouraging.
4. Don't force anyone to participate, but do make sure everyone knows his or her input is welcome.
5. Relax. Do your homework and don't feel tense about the session. Give your best effort, and let the Lord take care of the rest.
6. Pray for each adult in the session that they will benefit from the study. Pray for yourself that God will assist you as you lead.

## ENCOURAGE GROUP MEMBERS . . .

- *To read.* Invite them to read the participant material prior to each session. This allows them to prepare their minds for the topic to be discussed that week.
- *To pray.* This allows them to prepare their hearts for what God wants to show them through the lesson.
- *To be open.* Be open to the lesson, the group members, and especially to God's leading.

# TELLING THE STORY OF GOD
## Scripture, Tradition, Reason and Experience

- - - - - - - - - - - - - - - - - - - - - - - - - - - - - -

**Focus Scriptures:** Luke 24:13-35

**Session Goal:** To help group members understand what the story of God is and the importance of understanding its message.

- - - - - - - - - - - - - - - - - - - - - - - - - - - - - -

## OPENING OUR MINDS

### Option 1

Invite your adults to think of the first word that comes to mind when they hear the word "Bible." Write these on a dry erase board. Then share the following definition from the Merriam-Webster's Collegiate Dictionary, Tenth Edition: *The sacred scriptures of Christians comprising the Old Testament and the New Testament.* A secondary definition: *A publication that is preeminent especially in authoritativeness or wide readership.*

- **Is the Bible more than a sacred book? Why or why not?**

Share with the group that:

1. The Bible is the Spirit-inspired written record revealing one message of who God is and how He wants to relate to people in ways that will bring salvation and peace to them.

2. The Bible is "salvation history."

3. The Bible is the Spirit-inspired written revelation of God, who lovingly calls us to respond to His love by faith that leads to salvation and eternal life.

## Option 2

Go around the room and ask your group to complete this sentence: *If there were no Bible, then . . .* Follow up by asking,

- **What difference would it make to people and society in general if there were no Bible?**
- **Considering the Bible is thousands of years old, why should we study the Bible today? How is its message still relevant today?**

# OPENING THE WORD

## *Understanding Luke 24:13–35*

On the first Sunday of the resurrection two of Jesus' followers were traveling from Jerusalem to the village of Emmaus. These two travelers were discussing what had just happened (24:14). They were trying to make some sense of Jesus' betrayal, arrest, suffering, and crucifixion. They were confused and most likely experiencing a flood of emotions. Then, "Jesus himself came near and went with them" (v. 15.), but they were kept from recognizing Him. After hearing their story, He "interpreted to them the things about himself in all the scriptures . . . beginning with Moses and all the prophets" (v. 27). They invite the "stranger" to eat with them and talk further. During the meal their eyes were opened and they recognized Jesus. At that moment he disappears. They immediately return to Jerusalem and tell the Eleven of their encounter with the risen Savior.

Luke is more detailed about this encounter than Mark's account (16:12-13). It is clear that these two people, although followers, did not know the scripture and were slow to believe. This is why Jesus explains how His life, death, and resurrection was prophesied in Scripture and had in fact been fulfilled. Jesus, through the Spirit, continues to open the Scriptures to us and whose resurrection presence still set hearts on fire.

## *Option 1*

Begin by asking your group to close their eyes and imagine that they are followers of Jesus and they have just witnessed His crucifixion and death. Ask your group to silently consider what they might be thinking and how they might be feeling.

Read Luke 24:13-35.

- How do you think Jesus' followers felt after His death?
- Do you think they fully understood all that had happened? Why or why not?
- Why do you think they did not recognize Jesus?
- According to verses 19-24, how did they interpret Jesus' death and all that had occurred?
- How did Jesus respond? Why do you think He used the truth of Scripture to address their unbelief and hopelessness?
- Why do you think they asked Jesus to eat with them?
- After recognizing it was Jesus, in what ways did their encounter with Him effect their lives?

## Option 2

Divide everyone into groups of three. Ask each group to read Luke 24:13-35 and discuss what stands out to them from this story. After sufficient time, invite each group to share their discussion. Then ask,

- How do you think the followers were feeling at the beginning of the story?
- Why did Jesus use Scripture to address their unbelief and confusion?
- How do you think the followers were feeling at the end of the story?
- If you were to paraphrase this story for someone who had never heard it before, what would you say? How do you explain its message for us today?

## Imaginative Option

Read Luke 24:13-35 dramatically. Ask for a volunteer to be the narrator. Then, ask for volunteers to portray each of the followers and Jesus. As the narrator reads the story, the volunteers act out the story. Follow up by asking the questions from *Option 1*.

# OPENING OUR HEARTS

Share with the group that Jesus used Scripture to open the eyes of His followers to the truth of who He is. God gave us the Bible to provide us with the illumination and instruction we need, not only to live here on earth, but to inherit eternal life through Jesus Christ. It is the supreme authority in matters of faith and conduct.

During the time of John Wesley (1703-1791), it was typical for theologians to acknowledge the importance of church *tradition* and human *reason* to help us to read the *Scriptures* rightly. Wesley certainly agreed with this, but he also cleared a significant place for spiritual *experience*. These four elements have become known as "the Wesleyan quadrilateral." Today's story of the resurrected Jesus and His followers helps to make the point that these elements of *Scripture*, *tradition*, *reason*, and *experience* are deeply intertwined. When it comes to the message of the Bible, these elements used together can help us better understand God's Word.

- **Scripture** is the *primary* source for Christian doctrine. This asks, "What does God's Word say?"
- **Tradition** is seeing how faith through the past centuries has grown and developed. This asks, "How did past Christians, theologians, and Bible scholars interpret this passage?"
- **Experience** is understanding faith in the light of his or her own life. This asks, "How do past experiences help me understand this passage?"
- **Reason** helps understand faith through discerning and rational thought. This asks, "In what ways can I understand this passage logically?"

Ask,

- **How is *Scripture*, *tradition*, *reason*, and *experience* part of today's story?**
- **In what ways would you use *Scripture*, *tradition*, *reason*, and *experience* to understand today's story? How would you employ these in your Bible reading?**

- **Why is it important to read and understand the message of God's Word? Why is it important to share the message of God's Word with others?**

Close by writing the following acrostic on a dry erase board and discuss its meaning.

**W**orship and Bible reading go together.

**E**valuate difficult scripture by plainer scripture.

**S**tudy with other Christians.

**L**iving Word, not just written Word.

**E**xperiences are understood in light of Scripture.

**Y**es to what God asks us to do.

**A**pply Scripture to life—always.

**N**o limits on what grace can do in us.

# *Connect*

## WEEK I

*Telling the Story of God: Scripture, Tradition, Reason and Experience*

THIS WEEK: We will examine the ways to read and understand God's Word.

THINK ABOUT THIS: In what ways does God speak to you through His Word?

PRAYER CONCERNS:

# THE GOD WHO CREATES
## And the Creation God Invites to Be

- - - - - - - - - - - - - - - - - - - - - - - - - - - - - -

**Focus Scriptures:** Genesis 1:1-28

**Session Goal:** To help group members understand God is the Creator of the heavens and the earth.

- - - - - - - - - - - - - - - - - - - - - - - - - - - - - - - - -

## OPENING OUR MINDS

### Option 1

Read the each statement below and ask group members to reflect on its meaning. Then follow up by asking the corresponding question to each statement.

- *In the beginning . . .* **What thoughts do you have about how all things came into existence?**
- *God as Creator:* **How does understanding God as the creator affect your faith?**
- *Heavens and Earth:* Take time to think about the heavens and nature around you. **What thoughts and feelings do you have knowing God created all you see?**

Follow up by asking,

- **What are the influences that affect the way you understand the beginning of the created world?**
- **How do people know God in relationship to creation?**
- **What is the importance of acknowledging God as Creator to our faith?**

## Option 2

Before class print the following statement from the Apostles' Creed on a piece of paper: *"I believe in God the Father almighty, Creator of heaven and earth."* Make enough copies for each group member. Share with the group that the Apostles' Creed was a statement of faith that was created around 390 AD. The purpose of this creed was to make a statement of the basic Christian doctrines.

- **Why would this be included as an early statement of faith?**

Share with the group that people's opinions and ideas about how the heavens and earth came into existence vary. Both scientists and Bible scholars have studied and written books about how the universe and all that is in it came into being. Many spend their entire lives studying the "how," but today we are going to talk about the "who" regarding the beginning of it all.

Ask:

- **What might be a view a person would have about how creation began?**
- **Why is there so much debate about how the universe began?**

# OPENING THE WORD

## *Understanding Genesis 1:1-28*

"In the beginning . . ." (Genesis 1:1) are familiar words to most within the Christian world. The Bible begins with the story of how all came into being and begins the Story of God. This is not God's beginning; but the beginning of all that was created (the universe, plants, animals, humankind, and so on). We do not know what was before this point in time, but we do know our beginning and all that came into being. The Bible proclaims that the world and all that is in it did not happen by accident or through a series of random events. God created, period. This affirms to the Christian faith that there is no mystery when it comes to the "who" of creation and how all things came into existence. We see that God is eternal, before all that is. God is therefore separate from creation. That is, we recognize God as the maker and creator of the universe above all that has been created.

Genesis means "beginning," and this book of the Bible is the first . . . the beginning of God's Story to us. Scripture bears witness to a God who speaks—and that God's speech calls the universe into being. In Genesis, it is the speaking of God, the meaningful arranging of divine words, that begins the story of all creation. In reading or hearing Scripture, we find ourselves invited into that story.

## Option 1

Have a volunteer read Genesis 1:1-28. (Considering the amount of verses, you may want to break up the reading among several volunteers.) Share with the group that these verses begin the recorded Story of God to us. They do not tell us what happened before this time and there is no explanation of who God is . . . God exists.

- **What do these verses tell us about God?**
- **How do these verses set Christianity apart from all other beliefs about how the world came into being?**
- **Why is it important to acknowledge God as the Creator?**
- **What difference does it make that we believe that things didn't happen by chance, but were through divine design?**
- **Do you agree that if we say God is the Creator, then we recognize God as the Supreme Being over all? Why?**
- **What does it mean that we were created in the "image of God"?**
- **In what ways are we to "rule" over creation?**

## Option 2

Divide everyone into seven groups. Assign each group a passage and invite them to discuss their thoughts and feelings regarding the message of the verses they are given.

1. Genesis 1:1-5
2. Verses 6-10
3. Verses 11-13
4. Verses 14-19
5. Verses 20-23
6. Verses 24-25
7. Verses 26-28

Follow up by asking each group to read their passage and share their discussion.

- **What is the message, or messages, from these verses?**

# OPENING OUR HEARTS

## Option 1

Share with the group that opinions regarding creation can be conflict-ridden. Even Christians can be in disagreement regarding how the heavens and earth came into being. In light of the dividing tendency of this topic it is important that Christians think clearly and deeply about the issue of creation. The following beliefs offer a balanced and informed perspective on creation:

- *God created the world and all that is in it.*
- *Explanations that deny God as Creator are inadequate.*
- *Creation expresses the purpose of God in the world and we should not be preoccupied with every detail of the "how" when it comes to the origin of the world.*
- *All that is depends upon the Creator God.*
- *Human beings are created by God to 'image' God, to reflect the God who has been revealed as self-emptying love through Jesus Christ.*

Close by asking group members to silently think about ways believing "God as Creator" impacts their lives.

## Option 2

From Genesis to Revelation, the Bible tells an overarching story that stretches from creation all the way to the dawning of the age to come. It is our calling as Christians to proclaim and to live that story faithfully.

- **Why does the Bible start with the creation story?**
- **How does this story impact our lives today?**
- **In what ways does this story call us to a live a life committed to following God?**
- **In what ways can we share this story with others?**

# Connect

**WEEK 2**

*The God Who Creates: And the Creation God Invites to Be*

THIS WEEK: We will discuss the significance of acknowledging God as Creator.

THINK ABOUT THIS: How does the creation story impact the way you live?

PRAYER CONCERNS:

# THE TRAGEDY OF GOD'S STORY
## The Doctrine of Sin

**Focus Scriptures:** Genesis 3:19-24; Romans 6:20-23

**Session Goal:** To help group members understand the seriousness of sin.

## OPENING OUR MINDS

*Option 1*

Begin by reading the following scenarios and asking the group to respond what they believe the possible consequences to the following actions would be.

- o Rick continuously speaks negatively to his wife.
- o Sarah has been chatting with a coworker online and her husband is unaware of their communication.
- o Tim and Sherrie have been sexually active.
- o Tina lies to her boss about a work project.
- o Steve spreads gossip about his ex-girlfriend.

- **Do our actions always have consequences? Why or why not?**

Today we are going to look at the effect the actions (the sin) of the first man and woman had on themselves and the created world.

*Option 2*

Begin the session by asking people how they would define the word "sin."

- **Why do people choose to follow self rather than following God?**
- **How does a person's sin affect more than just themselves?**
- **Could our world ever become less sinful than it is now?**
- **What is the world's remedy for sin? What is God's remedy for sin?**

# OPENING THE WORD

## *Understanding Genesis 3:19-24; Romans 6:20-23*

Sin has consequences. It leaves a wake of destruction in its path that destroys and hurts all who encounter it. Sin is about death, but God is about life. God creates and sustains life; sin causes destruction and leads to death. Death and life cannot coexist at the same time. Something is either living or dead. This is true in the spiritual sense as well. Romans 6:23 says that the "wages of sin is death." Our sin causes a spiritual death within us and makes no room for a godly life. However, the second part of Romans 6:23 says, "but the gift of God is eternal life through Jesus Christ." Although sin leads to death, God, through Jesus Christ, offers life. When we turn from our sin and follow God and His Word, there is no room for death and the life of God reigns within us.

Adam and Eve were barred from the Garden and could not "take from the tree of life and eat and live forever" (vv. 22-23). Through Christ, we are offered redemption and the right to life. In the end, those who have trusted in Christ will be given access to the tree of life and able to enter the city of God and dwell with God forever (Revelation 22:14).

## *Option 1*

Begin by sharing with your group that all living things have a beginning (birth) and an end (death). People, plants, and animals have a starting point and a finish point. This is just a part of our human existence.

- **What are your thoughts and feelings when you hear the word *death*?**
- **What are your thoughts and feelings when you hear the word *life*?**

Ask a volunteer to read Genesis 3:19-24. Then, share that God created the perfect world and called it good. God created man and woman to enjoy creation and live in harmony. However, when they sinned they hid from God and damaged their relationship with God. It also caused a barrier between each other, humankind. The immediate consequences were that the woman would have pain in child birth and man would have to toil the earth for food.

- **Do you think that Adam and Eve were created to live forever? If so, why?**
- **Why do you think death/mortality was a consequence for their sin? Was this the only consequence?**
- **How does sin place a barrier between us and God?**

We read in Genesis 3:7 that after the man and woman sinned they realized they were naked and in 3:20 we read that God clothed them.

- **What does this tell us about God?**
- **Why do you think God banished them from the Garden?**

Read Romans 6:20-23. Ask:

- **In what ways does sin bring death, both physically and spiritually?**
- **In what ways does God bring life, both physically and spiritually?**
- **Why is eternal life a gift from God?**

## Option 2

Divide your group in half. Assign Group 1 Genesis 3:14-24 and Group 2 Romans 6:20-23. Ask Group 1 to read their passage and write down all the things they observe from the story. Ask Group 2 to write down 2-3 things they observe from their passage. After allowing enough time, bring the groups together and have them share their findings.

Ask:

- **In what ways does sin bring death, both physically and spiritually?**
- **In what ways does God bring life, both physically and spiritually?**

# OPENING OUR HEARTS

## Option 1

Because God created humankind with free will, we have the freedom to choose self or God. When we chose self, we place a barrier between ourselves and God. When we disobey God, we open the door for spiritual death; that is, separation from God. However, God sent His Son, Jesus Christ, to shed His blood on the cross to atone for our sins. That is, Christ's death bridged the division between humankind and God caused by sin. Repentance (being sorry and turning from our sin) and belief in Christ's death for our sins are necessary to restore a right relationship with God.

Close by asking your group to get quiet before God. Invite them to silently consider the following,

- **Is there anything in your life that is placing a barrier between you and God?**
- **Are there thoughts and actions that need to be confessed and forgiven of by God?**
- **This week I need God to help me . . .**

## Option 2

Life is a gift from God. To receive this gift, we need to accept Christ into our life, turn from your sins and begin living a life that is pleasing to God. If you feel you have done things that God couldn't forgive, the good news is you haven't. God is willing to give you this free gift of life if you choose to accept it regardless of what you have done.

Close by asking your group to get silent before God. Then read this prayer. *God, I confess those things in my life that are not pleasing to You. I acknowledge Jesus Christ as Lord and Savior, the One who gave His life on the Cross and was raised from the dead to bring me life. I receive this gift of forgiveness and life that you have made possible through this sacrifice. May your power and presence reign in my heart. May your Spirit guide and direct the words that I say, the thoughts that I think, and things that I do. Today, I choose the life You offer. In Jesus' name I pray, Amen.*

## Connect

**WEEK 3**

*The Tragedy of God's Story: The Doctrine of Sin*

THIS WEEK: We will discuss the seriousness of sin and how dealing with it is a matter of life and death.

THINK ABOUT THIS: In what ways does sin lead to spiritual death?

PRAYER CONCERNS:

# THE PEOPLE OF ISRAEL IN GOD'S STORY
## The Doctrine of Covenants

--------------------------------------------

**Focus Scriptures:** Genesis 12:1-9; Galatians 3:6-9

**Session Goal:** To help group members understand the importance of God's covenants.

--------------------------------------------

## OPENING OUR MINDS

*Option 1*

Begin by asking your group to respond to the following:

- **What are choices we make every day?**
- **How do you feel when you are chosen for something?**
- **Have you ever been chosen by someone to do something special or out of the ordinary?**

Choices are something we make everyday. Some choices are bigger than others. Today we are going to look at the calling of Abram by God. God *chose* Abram to make a covenant with and to bestow a special blessing on his life and the life of his descendants.

## Option 2

Share the following definition of "covenant" with your group: "a covenant is an agreement between persons. God also makes covenants with people. He promises to help and be a friend to all those who obey Him."[1] God's covenants—God's promises. A covenant is an agreement between parties. In the Bible the word "covenant" refers to the agreements made between God and the children of Israel, as well as to the New Covenant fulfilled in Jesus Christ.

- **What are some of the covenants people make with others?**
- **Do people always do what they promise? Why?**
- **What are some covenants God made with His people?**

Covenants:

> ➤ God promised Noah and all creation not to cause a natural disaster in response to our disobedience.

> ➤ God sought Abram and called him out of all humanity to be the father of all nations and through him He would make a great nation.

> ➤ God made a covenant with Moses that He would be their God and they would be His people.

> ➤ God made a covenant with David that through his line he would continue God's kingdom and it was fulfilled in Christ.

---

1. J. Wesley Eby, ed. *A Dictionary of the Bible & Christian Doctrine in Everyday English* (Kansas City: Beacon Hill Press of Kansas City, 2004), 64.

# OPENING THE WORD

## *Understanding Genesis 12:1-9; Galatians 3:6-9*

God calls Abram to leave his country and go to a land that God will show Abram. This call and promise included making Abram a great nation, make his name great, bless those who bless him, and all people will be blessed through Abram (vv. 2-3).

Through this covenant God chose Abram to make a nation that God would bless and make himself known to. Through Abrams descendants would come the promised Messiah, Jesus Christ. Through Christ's life, death, and resurrection salvation is made possible for all who would accept and believe (1 Corinthians 15:1-4).

In this story of Abram we see God's plan for salvation. God offers the covenant (promises), Abram believes them, and it is counted to him for righteousness. It is God that begins the covenant and gives the blessings. This is the model of relationship we see between Christians and Christ and it is for this purpose we are called the 'sons of Abraham'…his spiritual descendants. God first reaches out to us and we respond in faith and obedience.

The Abrahamic covenant is important for us to understand as Christians because it points to the promise of a Redeemer through whom all nations would be blessed. In this covenant, and by sending Christ, God demonstrated His love and grace. Galatians 3:16 says, "He redeemed us in order that the blessing given to Abraham might come to the Gentiles through Christ Jesus, so that by faith we might receive the promise of the Spirit." This blessing that started with Abram continues to us today through Christ.

## Option 1

Read Genesis 12:1-9. Then ask:

- **What are three things you noticed about God in this story?**
- **How do you think Abram felt about his encounter with God?**
- **Do you think it was easy for Abram to take this step of faith? Why or why not?**
- **Why do you think Abram chose to obey God?**

God chose Abram to bless and bless other nations through. We notice that God promised:

1. To make Abram the father of a great nation and many nations.
2. To bless Abram and make him great.
3. To make Abram a blessing.
4. To bless those who bless him and curse those who curse him.
5. To give Abram and his descendants forever all the land he sees.

Read Galatians 3:6-9.

- **What was God's vision for the covenant He made with Abram?**
- **What does this covenant have to do with us today?**
- **How are we involved or part of this covenant that was made thousands of years ago?**

Abram's faith and obedience paved the way for the salvation of the whole world. Abram was part of God's plan for humanity's redemption through Christ. He is considered the spiritual father/grandfather of all believers. His faith and obedience is an example that each of us should follow. Even though our lives will not be the path for the salvation of the whole world, our relationship with God and our obedience to His Word may be the path by which others find a relationship with God.

Divide your group into pairs. Give each pair a Bible, pen/pencil, and piece of paper. Write the following words on a dry erase board: go, chosen, blessing, covenant, promise, faith, and righteousness. Invite each group to read Genesis 12:1-9 and Galatians 3:6-9 and to write down their thoughts and feelings about the word on the board as they relate to the Scripture passages.

## OPENING OUR HEARTS

*Option 1*

John Wesley wrote in his journal on August 6, 1775: *"I mentioned to the congregation another means of increasing serious religion, which has been frequently practiced by our forefathers and attended with eminent blessing; namely, the joining in a covenant to serve God with all our heart and with all our soul."* Wesley created a covenant service in order for participants to gain a deeper understanding of what it means to make a covenant with God.

Consider creating a covenant service that your group can commit, recommit, or affirm their lives to God. This service could include responsive readings, Scripture readings (consider using Deuteronomy 31:9-13; Jeremiah 31:31-34; Psalm 50; John15:1-8; and any other passages you would like to include), hymns/choruses, and prayers. (There are many examples online that could help you in deciding how to create your service.) Whatever you decide, make this a time of focusing in on God and our relationship to Him.

*Option 2*

Share with the group that God chose Abram to make His covenant with. God asked Abram to step out on faith and follow God's leading and He would make him a blessing. Then, invite students to silently reflect on the following:

- *I feel God's blessing when . . .*
- *I can bless others by . . .*
- *This week I will follow God's lead by . . .*

# *Connect* _____

## WEEK 4

*The People of Israel in God's Story: The Doctrine of Covenants*

THIS WEEK: We will be discussing the importance of God's covenants.

THINK ABOUT THIS: What promises does God make to us in His Word?

PRAYER CONCERNS:

# A NEW TWIST IN GOD'S STORY
## The Doctrine of Christ

**Focus Scriptures:** Philippians 2:5-11

**Session Goal:** To help group members understand our belief about Jesus Christ.

## OPENING OUR MINDS

*Option 1*

Begin by asking your class the following *Agree or Disagree* statements about Jesus Christ. After each statement is read, ask the class to indicate whether they agree or disagree with the statement.

**Agree or Disagree?**

- *There was nothing special about the birth of Jesus.*
- *Jesus was a human, just like you and me.*
- *Jesus never sinned.*
- *Jesus died on the Cross for the sins of the world.*
- *Jesus rose from the dead.*
- *Right now, Jesus is in heaven.*
- *It doesn't really matter what you believe about Jesus; only that you believe He existed and make an effort to follow His teachings.*

## Option 2

Ask your group to think about what makes each of the following persons below unique. In other words, what sets them apart in history? You may even want to ask the group how each has impacted the world.

*Buddha*—was a sage born somewhere between the sixth and fourth century BC and on whose teachings Buddhism was founded.

*Muhammad*—The founder of Islam and is considered by Muslims as the last messenger and prophet of Allah. Today there are 1.4 billion Muslims world-wide who follow his teachings.

*Jesus Christ*—Christians believe that He is the Messiah whose coming was foretold in the Old Testament and that He died on a cross for our sins and was raised from the dead.

Follow up by asking:

- **Does it matter what we believe about someone?**
- **What about someone who we place our trust and faith?**
- **What sets Jesus Christ a part from all others who have ever lived?**

# OPENING THE WORD

## Understanding Philippians 2:5-11

Paul gives a clear Christology within these verses. He narrates the story of Christ so that followers will embody His pattern. Within this passage we find Paul making specific claims about Jesus: 1. He is God; 2. He was Man (the God-Man); 3. He came as a servant; 4. He died on the cross; and God raised Him from the dead; 5. He is worthy of everyone's worship and praise.

These words written in a letter to the church at Philippi have been viewed as a poem, a hymn, and a confession by Paul—the main focus being on Christ's humiliation (vv. 6-8) and exaltation (vv. 9-11).

From statements of these verses we understand that Jesus, being God, laid aside His glory and took human form—being fully human and fully divine. Jesus, in obedience to the Father, became a servant, humbled himself, and died on the cross. God raised Jesus from the dead and exalted Him to the highest place so that the world will acknowledge Jesus as Lord.

## Option 1

Read Philippians 2:5-11 several times and invite your group to think about the message of these words.

Reread verse 5.

- **What is Paul saying in this verse?**
- **What does it mean to have the "same mindset as Christ Jesus"?**

Reread verses 6-7.

- **What do these verses say about Jesus?**
- **In what ways did Jesus take the "very nature of a servant"?**

- **What does it mean that Jesus was both "in very nature God" and "made in human likeness"?**

Reread verses 8-9.

- **Why did Jesus humble himself and willingly go to the cross?**
- **In what ways did God exalt Jesus?**
- **What does it mean that Jesus' "name is above every name"?**

Reread verses 10-11.

- **What do you think it means that "every knee should bow" and "every tongue acknowledge" that Jesus is Lord?**
- **Do you think there will be a day when *every* person will acknowledge Jesus is Lord?**
- **Why is it important to acknowledge Jesus is Lord?**
- **In what ways can these verses guide us in our relationship with those of other faiths and beliefs?**

**If someone were to ask you the meaning of verses 6-11, what would you say?**

## Option 2

Break everyone into four groups. Assign each group one of the following passages: Matthew 1:20-25; Romans 8:3, 32-34; Philippians 2:5-11; and 1 John 1:1-3. Give each group a piece of paper and pen/pencil. Instruct each group to look up their assigned passage and write down all the things that the passage says about Jesus.

Share with the group that our beliefs about Jesus come from who the Bible says He was and is. He was more than just a great teacher; He was truly the Son of God who died for our sins and rose again for the salvation of the world. He ascended into heaven and is in intercession for us even now.

# OPENING OUR HEARTS

## Option 1

Ask the group to respond to the following questions:

- **Does having a biblical belief about Jesus really matter? If so, why?**
- **What is the danger of believing something other than what the Bible says about Jesus?**
- **How does what we believe about Jesus affect our daily lives?**

Wrap up the session by using the statements below to summarize the beliefs about Jesus you have studied today.

- *He has always existed as part of the Trinity—God the Son.*
- *He was born of a virgin and lived on earth fully human and fully divine.*
- *He died on a cross for the sins of humankind.*
- *God raised Him from the dead.*
- *He ascended into heaven and is in intercession for us.*

## Option 2

Share with the group that Jesus was the Son of God, who came to earth, died and was raised. In light of this, God exalted Him so "that in the name of Jesus every knee should bow and that every tongue should confess that Jesus Christ is Lord to the glory of God, the Father" (Philippians 2:10-11).

Read Ephesians 1:20-23, "*he exerted when he raised Christ from the dead and seated him at his right hand in the heavenly realms, far above all rule and authority, power and dominion, and every name that is invoked, not only in the present age but also in the one to come. And God placed all things under his feet and appointed him to be head over everything for the church, which is his body, the fullness of him who fills everything in every way.*" Then, invite everyone to get quiet before God. Lead your group in prayer, praising Jesus for who He is and what He has done and is doing.

## *Connect*

**WEEK 5**

*A New Twist in God's Story: The Doctrine of Christ*

THIS WEEK: We will examine what the Bible says about Jesus.

THINK ABOUT THIS: If someone were to ask you about Jesus, what would you say?

PRAYER CONCERNS:

# LIVING IN GOD'S STORY
## The Doctrine of the Church

**Focus Scriptures:** Acts 2:42-47

**Session Goal:** To help group members understand the importance and role of the Church.

## OPENING OUR MINDS

### Option 1

Start this session by asking your group to complete the following statements:

- *The Church is....*
- *Characteristics of the Church are...*
- *The Church exists because...*

Follow up by asking for a volunteer to share how he or she decided to attend this local Church and how it has impacted his or her life.

### Option 2

Begin by asking your group to respond to the following scenarios.

- **In conversation with a co-worker, this person makes the comment that he or she does not go to Church because it is full of hypocrites and all they do is ask for money. You politely disagree. This person responds by saying, "Okay, what do you think the Church is?" What would you say?**

- A friend recently moved to a city several states away from you. He is looking for a church and asks you what he should look for when deciding on where he and his family will attend. What would you tell him?

- Your preteen is beginning to ask a lot of questions about her God, her faith, and the church. Recently she asked you why the church is called "the body of Christ"? How would you explain this to her?

- You and several church members are watching the news together. The broadcast reports on the high number of homeless in your community. One person comments that your church could raise money to help these people. However, another person feels we pay taxes for government agencies to help these people and should rely on them to help the homeless. How do you respond?

## Understanding Acts 2:42-47

After Jesus ascended to heaven, there were many who remained faithful to the mission of Christ. In chapter 2 the Holy Spirit came and fell upon a group of believers and Peter preached the message of good news to the masses gathered there. Peter called for people to repent and be baptized. Three thousand that day turned their hearts toward God.

We read what happens to this group in Acts 2:42-47. These believers are the early Church. As soon as people became part of the community of faith they "devoted themselves to the apostles teachings and to the fellowship of the breaking of bread, and to prayer" (Acts 2:42). They also sold their possessions to help those in need and met together daily, praising God (vv. 46-47). God's Spirit was moving and people were becoming followers each day.

We come to God individually, but we live the Christian life in community. One of the most common terms for the Church is the "body of Christ"—different parts making the whole. Immediately after Pentecost (Acts 2:1-41), the people gathered together and began to become a community of believers (vv. 42-47). They studied God's Word, ministered to others, praised God, and ate together in fellowship. These things are still the foundation of the Church today.

## Option 1

Share with your group that Jesus ascended into heaven and His followers began preaching the "good news" to others. A group of Jesus' followers gathered, and the Holy Spirit came and filled these people with God's presence. Peter began to preach to the crowd gathered there and three thousand people came to faith in Christ—the Church begins.

Invite a volunteer to read Acts 2:42-47.

- **What were the characteristics of the early Church?**
- **Why is teaching important in the Church?**
- **Why is fellowship important in the Church?**
- **Why is preaching/sharing our faith important in the Church?**
- **Why is giving to the needy important in the Church?**
- **Why is praising God important in the Church?**

Write on a dry erase board the words teaching, fellowship, preaching, giving, and praising God. Space them out so that they are not directly beneath or above each other. Draw lines from one word to the other. Ask group members how they think all these things work together in the ministry of the Church.

## Option 2

Divide everyone into groups of three. Give each group a piece of paper and pen/pencil. Instruct each group to read Acts 2:42-47, and then to re-write this passage using modern-day language. That is, re-write this as if the event took place today. Allow groups sufficient time to work, and then have each group share their work. Take time to discuss how the early Church set the standard and pattern for us in the Church today.

# OPENING OUR HEARTS

## Option 1

The Church is often referred to as the "body of Christ." Just as a body is made up of many parts, so to the body of Christ is made up of different people with different gifts and abilities. Each part works together to make the body move. The Church is the body and Christ is the head. As followers of Christ, we work together, empowered by the Holy Spirit, to be the hands and feet of Christ in the world. Invite students to think about their place in the Church. Then, read the statements below, pausing between each one to allow students to reflect on their silent response.

- *Fellowship*—In what ways am I actively involved in building relationships with others in my community of faith?
- *Teaching*—In what ways am I committing myself to learning more about God and growing in my faith?
- *Sharing Our Faith*—In what ways am I sharing my faith with others?
- *Giving*—In what ways am I giving myself to the work and ministry of helping others?
- *Worship/Praise*—In what ways am I involved in the community of faith's worship and praise of God?

## Option 2

Ask your group to think of one way they could be the hands and feet of Christ this week. (These might include prayer, active worship, act of kindness, sharing your faith, and being involved in a ministry.) Give each person a slip of paper and ask them to write down one or two things as a reminder of what they have committed to. Close by reciting this prayer together.

*Sovereign God—Father, Son, and Holy Spirit,*
*We come before you as the community of faith and ask for your guidance and strength to be your hands and feet in the world. May we be faithful to your calling of giving our lives in service to you. We commit our lives to the empowering work of your Holy Spirit and ask that you would direct the words we say and the things we do. May we live as the body of Christ in our world. In Jesus name we pray, Amen.*

# *Connect* ----------------------------------

## WEEK 6

### *Living in God's Story: The Doctrine of the Church*

THIS WEEK: We will talk about the Church and why it is called the body of Christ.

THINK ABOUT THIS: What makes the Church the body of Christ?

PRAYER CONCERNS:

# THE END OF GOD'S STORY
## The Doctrine of Last Things

**Focus Scriptures:** 1 Corinthians 15:12-58; Revelation 20:11-15

**Session Goal:** To help group members understand what the Bible says about last things.

## OPENING OUR MINDS

### Option 1

Begin your session by reading each phrase. Allow group members to reflect on each phrase, and then ask them to respond to the question following the statement.

- o *"Kingdom of God"* What is the kingdom of God?
- o *"Present kingdom"* How is the kingdom of God a present reality?
- o *"Future kingdom"* How is the kingdom of God to be a future anticipation?

- **What do Christians believe about the return of Christ and the end of the world?**
- **In what ways does our belief in Christ's return affect the way we live?**

## Option 2

Begin the class by showing a clip from the movie *The Day After Tomorrow*. Find the clip where Professor Rapson and Jack are charting the direction of the coming storm. As they talk, Rapson contemplates the magnitude of the storm and the way it will affect his life.

After the clip ask:

- **Do you think people worry about the end of their life? Why, or why not?**
- **What would you do if you knew the end of the world was next week? How would it change your life?**
- **Should we live everyday as if it could be our last day on earth? Why or why not?**

# OPENING THE WORD

## *Understanding 1 Corinthians 15:12-58; Revelation 20:11-15*

Paul writes in 1 Corinthians 15 that just as Jesus was raised from the dead, so to, we (each person who has ever lived) who have died will someday rise from the dead. The power that raised Christ is also the power that will raise the dead. Each person, both believers and unbelievers, will rise on the day Christ returns. On that day, both the living and the dead who have been raised will face God and be judged according to how they have lived. Those who have followed Christ will live eternally with God and those who have rejected God will be separated from Him forever (Revelation 20:11-15).

Just as it was in the beginning, God will again bring the world back to perfection. When Christ returns, both the living and the dead will be judged and God will create a new heaven and earth, with God as King. Sin and its destruction will no longer exist. God will establish the perfect world, where those who have faithfully served Him will live in perfect relationship with their Creator. As it was in the Garden, the world will again be perfect.

## *Option 1*

Before your session, write the following on three separate 3x5 index cards.

*Card 1: 1 Corinthians 15:12-34*

- **What do these verses say about the resurrection?**
- **What do these verses say about God?**
- **If you were to summarize these verses in 2-3 sentences, what would you say?**
- **How is the message of these verses good news?**

*Card 2: 1 Corinthians 15:35-58*

- **What do these verses say about the resurrection?**

- **What do these verses say about those living at the end of time?**
- **What do these verses say about death?**
- **If you were to summarize these verses in 2-3 sentences, what would you say?**
- **How is the message of these verses good news?**

*Card 3: Revelation 20:11-15*

- **What do these verses say about the destiny of humankind?**
- **If you were to summarize these verses in 2-3 sentences, what would you say?**
- **How is the message of these verses good news?**

Divide everyone into three groups. Give each group one card and pen/pencil. Instruct each group to read the passage and answer the questions. After sufficient time, ask each group to read their passage and share their discussion.

## Option 2

Invite your pastor to come and share with your group what your church believes about end things such as Jesus' return, the resurrection of the dead, and eternal destiny. Be sure he/she allows for group members to ask questions. Follow-up by reading 1 Corinthians 15:12-58 and Revelation 20:11-15 and discussing how these passages relate to what the pastor has shared and talked about with your group

# OPENING OUR HEARTS

## Option 1

The Bible tells us that Christ's return will include these events:

1. *The Heavenly Father, will determine when the appropriate time arrives.*
2. *He will signal Jesus, to return bodily to earth accompanied by a host of angels.*
3. *Jesus will appear in the eastern sky, visible to believers and nonbelievers.*
4. *His return will mark the end of time as we know it.*

5. *Resurrection, judgment, and eternal reward or punishment will await everyone who has ever lived on earth.*[2]

Follow up by asking:

- **How important is belief in Christ's return to believers? How important is belief in Christ's return to nonbelievers?**
- **Why is it important that we live every day in obedience to God and His Word?**
- **Why do you think Jesus has not returned yet?**

As a way to close this lesson and this study, read the Apostles' Creed together. Remind students that this is a statement of the Christian faith. Encourage students to think about each statement as you recite this creed as a group.

### Apostles' Creed

*I believe in God, the Father Almighty,*
*the Maker of heaven and earth,*
*and in Jesus Christ, His only Son, our Lord:*

*Who was conceived by the Holy Ghost,*
*born of the virgin Mary,*
*suffered under Pontius Pilate,*
*was crucified, dead, and buried;*

*He descended into hell.*

*The third day He arose again from the dead;*

*He ascended into heaven,*
*and sits on the right hand of God the Father Almighty;*
*from thence he shall come to judge the quick and the dead.*

*I believe in the Holy Ghost;*
*the holy catholic church;*
*the communion of saints;*

2. *Articles of Faith: a Small-group study* (Kansas City: WordAction Publishing Co., 2008), 38.

*the forgiveness of sins;*
*the resurrection of the body;*
*and the life everlasting.*

*Amen.*

## Option 2

During this 7-week study you have examined the Story of God. As a way to close this study, ask the following questions:

- **What is one thing you learned over the course of these seven weeks?**
- **In what ways has this study strengthened your relationship with God?**
- **In what ways has this study strengthened your relationship with others?**

Close by inviting your group to get quiet before God. Ask each person to thank God for His message to us through His Word.

# Connect - - - - - - - - - - - - - - - - - - - - - - - - - - - - - -

## WEEK 7

*The End of God's Story: The Doctrine of Last Things*

THIS WEEK: We will discuss what the Bible says about last things.

THINK ABOUT THIS: In what ways are you living in anticipation of Christ's return?

PRAYER CONCERNS:

*Other Dialog studies also available!*

## THE BEATITUDES
*Living a Blessed Life*

Discover why those who live as described in
the Beatitudes are likely to find themselves
both at odds with, and misunderstood
by, cultures built on radically different
assumptions.

PARTICIPANT'S GUIDE ISBN 978-0-8341-3374-7
FACILITATOR'S GUIDE ISBN 978-0-8341-3373-0

## THE PROPHETS
*Hearing the Timeless Voice of God*

The prophets live during specific times
and speak specific words to their listeners.
Yet, because their messages are from God,
their words are timeless. Learn about seven
of these prophets, who they are, and the
messages they deliver that transcend time to
grow your spirit today.

PARTICIPANT'S GUIDE ISBN 978-0-8341-3376-1
FACILITATOR'S GUIDE ISBN 978-0-8341-3375-4

**Available online at DialogSeries.com**